God gave you a Power

Dorothy J. Szypulski

Illustrations by Mitzie Stone

God Gave You A Power by Dorothy J. Szypulski

ISBN: 978-1-59755-341-4

Published by: ADVANTAGE BOOKS™
www.advbookstore.com

Cover Design by Robin E. Szypulski

Illustrations by Mitzie Stone

Also available as an eBook (ISBN:978-1-59755-347-6)

First Printing: September 2013
13 14 15 16 17 18 19 10 9 8 7 6 5 4 3 2 1
Printed in the United States of America

To Ted, Laura and Robin for their unyielding faith in me, and to Charles Payne, whose perseverance and courage inspired me to write this book.

"Give and gifts will be given to you; a good measure, packed together, shaken down, and overflowing, will be poured into your lap. For the measure with which you measure will in return be measured out to you." (Luke 6: 38)

When God created each one of us, he gave us our own special talents, skills and abilities. They are usually the things we most enjoy doing. You may have a beautiful singing voice, but your best friend sings like a frog with a bad cold. On the other hand, your friend might be able to paint perfectly, but you have trouble staying in the lines when coloring a picture. If this is the case, then your gift is music and your friend's gift is art. Whatever your talent is, it is special to you and it is part of what makes you unique.

God gave us these gifts so we can use them for our world. A skill or a talent is like a POWER because we can use it to help others. God wants each of us to use our power to do good things and to be good people, but first we must practice using our powers. We must work at our skills and then, when we are ready, we can use them in our world.

What is your gift? What is your special Power?

If today you practice your special Power
to build a bridge…

…then one day you might use your special Power
to bring people together

If today you practice your special Power
to color pictures

...then one day soon you might use your special Power
to color our neighborhoods.

If today you practice your special Power
to add and subtract…

...then one day you might use your special Power
to help others save their money!

If today you practice your special Power
to help your friend...

...then one day you might use your special Power
to help someone learn to walk again!

If today you practice your special Power
to help others to be safe...

...then one day you might use your special Power
to keep a whole city safe!

If today you practice your special Power
to sing your best...

...then one day you might use your special Power
to give joyous music to the world!

If today you practice your special Power
to study science…

...then one day you might use your special Power
to find cures and save lives!

If today you practice your special Power
to write a story...

...then one day you might use your special Power
to inspire others with your stories!

If today you practice your special Power
to understand how things work...

...then one day you might use your special Power
to help others travel the world!

If today you practice your special Power
to stitch together fabrics...

...then one day you might use your special Power
to keep others warm and comfortable!

Do you know what your special Power is?

It is inside of you waiting to be used. What is your favorite thing to do? Whatever it is, stay with it and keep practicing. The world is waiting for you!

For more information contact:

Dorothy Szypulski
Advantage Books
PO Box 160847
Altamonte Springs, FL 32716

info@advbooks.com

To purchase additional copies of this book online, go to : www.advbookstore.com

Phone Orders call the ***Advantage Books*** order line at:

407-788-3110 (Book Orders Only)

Longwood, Florida, USA
"we bring dreams to life"™
www.advbooks.com

CPSIA information can be obtained at www.ICGtesting.com
Printed in the USA
LVOW02s1923090913

351684LV00001B/1/P